KENDRICK LAMAR:

Biography of a Kid with a Mic

Nicole D. Riggs

TABLE OF CONTENTS

A Kid from Compton

In the heart of California, just south of Los Angeles, there was a city that never stayed quiet. Compton was always alive with music, voices, and the sounds of everyday life. Cars rolled by with hip-hop beats blasting from their speakers, kids rode bikes down the sidewalks, and families gathered outside to talk and laugh. But Compton was also a place where life could be tough. Some streets were dangerous, and many families had to work extra hard just to get by.

In 1987, in this very city, a baby boy was born. His name was Kendrick Lamar Duckworth. His parents, Paula and Kenny, had moved to California from Chicago before he was born, hoping for a better future. They worked hard to take care of their family, making sure Kendrick and his siblings had food to eat and a roof over their heads. Life wasn't always easy, but their home was filled with love, lessons, and encouragement.

Kendrick grew up paying attention to everything around him. He saw the good and the bad, the struggles and the victories. He listened to the stories people told, watched how they moved, and noticed how music seemed to be everywhere. While some kids only heard the beats of hip-hop songs playing from passing cars, Kendrick felt them. It was as if the music was speaking to him, telling him stories that he needed to understand.

Even before he picked up a microphone, Kendrick picked up a notebook. As a kid, he loved words. He would sit quietly, filling pages with thoughts, rhymes, and poems. He didn't just write about himself, he wrote about what he saw in his neighborhood, what he felt in his heart, and the dreams he kept tucked away in his mind. At the time, he didn't know what all those words meant. He didn't know that they would one day turn into songs that millions of people would sing along to. He just knew that he loved to write, and he couldn't stop.

One of Kendrick's biggest inspirations was Tupac Shakur. Tupac wasn't just a rapper, he was a storyteller. His music wasn't just about fun; it was about real life. He rapped about struggle, hope, and fighting for a better future. When Kendrick listened to Tupac, he felt like he understood something deeper. Tupac's music made him feel like anything was possible, like he could take his own words and turn them into something powerful.

When Kendrick was about eight years old, he had a moment he would never forget. His father took him to see Tupac and Dr. Dre filming the music video for *California Love* right in the streets of Compton. Kendrick stood in the crowd, watching his hip-hop heroes perform, feeling the energy in the air. At that moment, something changed inside him. He wanted to do that. He wanted to tell stories, to make music, to be a voice that people listened to.

He didn't have a microphone yet, and he didn't have a stage. But he had his words. He had his dreams. And he had a city full of stories waiting to be told.

Even as a young boy, Kendrick knew that dreams didn't just come true on their own. If he wanted to make music, he would have to work hard. He would have to keep writing, keep listening, and keep believing in himself, even when things got tough. He was just a kid from Compton, but deep down, he felt like he was meant for something bigger.

And so, with a notebook full of rhymes and a heart full of ambition, Kendrick Lamar began a journey that would take him further than he ever imagined. This was only the beginning.

Chapter 1: Music in His Heart

From the moment Kendrick Lamar could remember, music was everywhere. It was in the streets of Compton, booming from passing cars. It was in his home, playing through the speakers while his parents danced and sang along. It was in his heart, beating along with every rhythm he heard. Even as a little boy, Kendrick felt that music wasn't just sound, it was emotion, a way to tell stories, a way to express something deeper than words alone.

His parents loved music, and they made sure Kendrick grew up hearing the best of it. His mom played old-school R&B and soul, the kind of music that made you feel something in your bones. His dad introduced him to funk and hip-hop, teaching him about beats and rhythm. But the music that hit Kendrick the hardest was rap. The way rappers put words together, the way their rhymes told stories, the way their voices carried so much power, it was like poetry, but with a beat.

Kendrick didn't just listen to songs; he studied them. He paid attention to how the words flowed, how the rhymes connected, how the beats made everything come to life. He listened to artists like Jay-Z, Nas, and The Notorious B.I.G., soaking in every verse, every line, every message. But no artist spoke to him like Tupac Shakur. Tupac wasn't just making music, he was teaching, sharing, and speaking truth. His words weren't just about fame and success; they were about struggle, hope, and fighting for something bigger than yourself.

Kendrick wanted to do that. He wanted to make music that mattered.

At school, while other kids were talking about their favorite basketball players or the newest video games, Kendrick was thinking about rhymes. He started writing down his thoughts in notebooks, filling page after page with lines that described what he saw, what he felt, and what he dreamed about. He didn't know it yet, but those words would one day turn into lyrics that would inspire the world.

Kendrick wasn't loud or flashy like some of the other kids. He was quiet, always thinking, always observing. But when it came to music, he felt alive. Whenever he heard a great song, he couldn't sit still. The beats made him want to move, the lyrics made him want to create, and the music made him feel like he belonged to something bigger.

One day, Kendrick got his first chance to step up to a microphone. He was just a teenager, but he had already filled notebooks with rhymes. He had been practicing, studying, and dreaming. Now, it was time to see if he had what it took.

When he heard his voice play back for the first time, it was like magic. The words he had written down, the thoughts he had kept to himself, were now alive in the form of music. It was a feeling like no other. It was as if, for the first time, the world could hear what had been in his heart all along.

From that moment on, Kendrick knew, music wasn't just something he loved. It was something he needed. It was his way of telling the world who he was, where he came from, and what he believed in. It was his way of turning his dreams into reality.

He wasn't famous yet. He wasn't on the radio or winning awards. But deep inside, he knew he was on the right path. He was just a kid from Compton with a mic in his hand and music in his heart, ready to share his voice with the world.

Chapter 2: Writing Rhymes, Chasing Dreams

Kendrick Lamar didn't just love music, he lived it. Every day, he filled pages of his notebook with rhymes, thoughts, and stories. He wrote about the streets of Compton, about what he saw and felt, about dreams that felt too big but too important to ignore. While other kids played basketball or video games for hours, Kendrick was busy with his words. To him, writing wasn't just a hobby. It was his way of making sense of the world.

He had listened to the greats, Tupac, Jay-Z, Nas, and Dr. Dre. He studied the way they rapped, how they put words together, how their lyrics flowed like poetry. He saw that hip-hop wasn't just about rhyming words, it was about storytelling. The best rappers didn't just rap; they painted pictures with their lyrics, making listeners feel like they were right there with them. That's what Kendrick wanted to do. He didn't want to rap just to sound cool, he wanted to tell stories that mattered.

At first, Kendrick kept his rhymes to himself. He was a quiet kid, more of an observer than a talker. But deep down, he knew he had something special. He just needed the courage to share it. Then, one day, he got his chance.

One of Kendrick's friends had access to a small recording studio, not a big fancy one like the ones on TV, but a simple setup where young artists could record their own songs. Kendrick stepped up to the microphone, nervous but excited. As the beat played, he took a deep breath and started rapping. The words he had written in his notebook flowed out of him, matching the rhythm of the music perfectly.

When he finished and heard his voice played back, he couldn't believe it. This was real. His rhymes weren't just in his notebook anymore, they were alive in a song. That moment changed everything. It made him believe that maybe, just maybe, he could turn this dream into something real.

After that first recording, Kendrick couldn't stop. He kept writing, kept practicing, and kept improving. He recorded more songs, shared them with friends, and started getting noticed. People were impressed. He wasn't just another kid trying to rap, he had something different. His lyrics had meaning, his voice had passion, and his stories felt real.

But chasing a dream wasn't easy. There were moments of doubt, moments when he wondered if he was good enough. He saw how hard it was to make it in the music industry, how many people tried and never got their big break. But Kendrick wasn't the type to give up. He had something inside him, determination, patience, and a belief that his words mattered.

Kendrick also knew he couldn't just rely on talent. He had to work harder than everyone else. So he studied even more. He wrote every single day, pushing himself to make his lyrics stronger, his flow smoother, his storytelling more powerful. He listened to beats and figured out how to make his words dance with the music.

His hard work started paying off. More people began to recognize his talent. He got the chance to work with other young artists in Compton, learning from them and improving his craft. He was still just a teenager, but he was already proving that he had something special.

And then, something big happened. Kendrick got the opportunity to record his very first mixtape, a collection of songs that would introduce him to the world. He poured everything he had into it, making sure every song was the best it could be. When he finally released it, people took notice. His music was raw, honest, and full of emotion. It wasn't just another mixtape, it was a glimpse into the mind of a young artist who had something real to say.

That first mixtape didn't make Kendrick famous overnight. He didn't suddenly become a superstar. But it was a start. It was proof that his dream wasn't just a dream, it was possible.

And so, Kendrick kept going. He kept writing, kept recording, and kept chasing his dream, one rhyme at a time.

Chapter 3: The Good Kid's Journey

Kendrick Lamar was different from many kids in Compton. He wasn't the loudest in the room, and he didn't try to act tough to impress others. He was thoughtful, quiet, and always paying attention. He was what some might call a "good kid" in a city that could be rough.

Growing up in Compton wasn't easy. The streets were full of distractions and dangers, gang violence, crime, and struggles that made life unpredictable. Kendrick saw it all. He knew kids who got caught up in trouble, kids who made choices that changed their lives forever. But he also knew that he wanted something different for himself.

He wasn't perfect. Like any teenager, he had moments of doubt and temptation. But deep down, he knew that his future was bigger than the streets. His parents had worked hard to give him a chance at something better, and he didn't want to waste it. He focused on school, listened to his family's advice, and most importantly, poured his heart into music.

Even when things around him felt chaotic, Kendrick used music as his escape. He wrote about what he saw, the good and the bad, the struggles and the victories. He didn't pretend that everything was perfect, but he also didn't let the tough times define him. Instead, he turned them into lessons.

As he started gaining recognition for his music, he realized something important, his words had power. His songs weren't just about him; they spoke for people who didn't always have a voice. He was telling the stories of his community, the struggles of young kids trying to find their way, and the hope that existed even in difficult times.

Kendrick's journey wasn't just about making music; it was about finding his place in the world. He knew he wanted to be more than just another rapper. He wanted to be a leader, an inspiration, a storyteller who could help others see that no matter where they came from, they had the power to create their own path.

The more he rapped, the more people listened. And the more people listened, the more he realized that he had a responsibility. He wasn't just rapping for fun anymore, he was speaking for a generation. He was proving that a "good kid" from Compton could rise above the challenges and achieve something great.

His journey was far from over, but he was ready for whatever came next. The good kid was on his way to changing the world, one song at a time.

Chapter 4: A Voice for the People

As Kendrick Lamar's talent grew, so did his audience. More and more people started listening to his music, and they weren't just hearing the beats, they were feeling the words. Kendrick wasn't rapping just to show off his skills. He was telling real stories about life in Compton, about struggle and survival, about dreams and determination. His music wasn't just entertainment; it was a message.

People connected with Kendrick because he wasn't afraid to be honest. He didn't pretend to be someone he wasn't. He didn't rap about things he didn't live. Instead, he shared his truth, the truth of a kid who grew up in a tough city but refused to let his surroundings define his future. His songs were raw, emotional, and full of meaning. They spoke to people who had been through the same struggles, who had felt the same pain, who had the same hopes for something better.

One of the first moments that proved Kendrick's music was bigger than just rap was when he released his mixtapes. Each one showed his growth, his talent, and his ability to turn everyday experiences into powerful lyrics. His words painted pictures of life in Compton, from the laughter of children playing in the streets to the sirens that echoed in the night. He wasn't glorifying the struggles, he was giving a voice to the people who lived them.

As his name spread, so did his influence. He started performing at bigger shows, meeting other artists, and gaining respect in the hip-hop world. But through it all, he stayed true to who he was. He didn't let fame change his message. Instead, he used his growing platform to speak even louder.

Kendrick's breakthrough came when he released his album *good kid, m.A.A.d city*. The album was more than just a collection of songs, it was a story. It told the tale of a young boy growing up in Compton, trying to navigate the challenges of his environment while holding onto his dreams. It was Kendrick's own story, but it was also the story of so many others.

The album was a massive success. People everywhere connected with it, from fans in Compton to listeners all over the world. Kendrick had proven that hip-hop could be more than just music, it could be a movement. His voice was powerful because it wasn't just his voice anymore. It was the voice of the people who had lived through the same struggles, the same fears, the same dreams.

With his rising fame, Kendrick could have chosen to focus only on success. He could have made music just to sell records. But that wasn't who he was. He wanted to make a difference. He wanted to inspire. He wanted to remind people, especially young kids like him, that they could rise above their circumstances.

Kendrick started speaking out about issues that mattered, poverty, violence, injustice, and the power of self-belief. He used his lyrics to challenge the world to pay attention, to listen, to understand. He wasn't just a rapper anymore; he was a leader, a storyteller, a voice for those who needed one.

As he stood on stages in front of thousands of fans, Kendrick knew that he had a responsibility. His words could inspire change. His music could give hope. And that was exactly what he was going to do.

The quiet kid from Compton had found his voice. And the world was listening.

Chapter 5: Winning Big, Staying Humble

Kendrick Lamar had come a long way from the quiet kid in Compton who filled notebooks with rhymes. His music was everywhere, on the radio, in people's headphones, and blasting from cars just like the songs he used to listen to as a kid. He was no longer just a rising rapper; he was one of the biggest names in hip-hop.

His album *good kid, m.A.A.d city* had changed everything. It was more than just a hit, it was a masterpiece that told a real, powerful story. Fans called it one of the best rap albums of all time, and critics agreed. People connected with the honesty in his lyrics, the storytelling, and the emotion he poured into every song. The album went platinum, selling millions of copies, and suddenly, Kendrick was on top of the music world.

But he wasn't done yet.

His next album, *To Pimp a Butterfly*, took his music even further. It wasn't just about his personal journey, it was about the struggles of an entire generation. The album was bold, powerful, and full of messages about race, identity, and justice. Songs like *Alright* became anthems for people fighting for change. The album won Grammy Awards, broke records, and cemented Kendrick's place as one of the greatest artists of his time.

More success followed. He released *DAMN.*, another groundbreaking album that won a Pulitzer Prize, the first time a rapper had ever received such an honor. The Pulitzer wasn't just about music; it was about storytelling, impact, and influence. Kendrick's words were bigger than hip-hop, they were poetry, history, and truth all at once.

With all of his success, Kendrick could have let fame change him. He could have lived in a mansion far away from where he started and left his old life behind. But that wasn't who he was.

Even with Grammy Awards, platinum albums, and millions of fans, Kendrick remained humble. He still carried himself like the quiet, observant kid from Compton who loved music and storytelling. He didn't show off or act like he was better than anyone else. Instead, he focused on his purpose, using his voice to inspire, to uplift, and to make a difference.

Whenever he won an award, he thanked his family, his city, and the people who supported him. He didn't just celebrate himself, he celebrated the journey, the lessons, and the struggles that made him who he was. He gave back to Compton, helping schools, charities, and young artists who had dreams just like he once did.

Despite all his achievements, Kendrick never forgot why he started. He didn't make music just for fame or fortune, he made music because it meant something. He rapped because he had a story to tell. And no matter how big he got, he never lost sight of that.

Through all the awards, the headlines, and the success, Kendrick Lamar remained the same at his core, a kid with a mic, a heart full of stories, and a message the world needed to hear.

Chapter 6: Inspiring the Next Generation

Kendrick Lamar had achieved what many could only dream of. He had gone from a kid writing rhymes in his notebook to one of the most respected artists in the world. His music had won awards, topped charts, and influenced millions. But for Kendrick, success wasn't just about personal achievement, it was about what he could give back.

He knew there were kids in Compton, and in cities just like it, who were growing up the same way he had. They had big dreams but faced big challenges. Some of them felt stuck, unsure if they could ever escape the struggles around them. Kendrick wanted to show them that they could. He wanted them to see that their voices mattered, that their stories were important, and that they had the power to create their own future.

One of the ways he gave back was through his community. He donated to schools, provided resources for young students, and supported programs that helped kids find their passion, whether it was music, sports, or education. He wanted to make sure that the next generation had the tools to succeed.

But Kendrick's biggest impact wasn't just in what he gave, it was in what he represented. He showed young people that they didn't have to change who they were to be successful. They didn't have to pretend to be someone else or follow a path that didn't feel right to them. They could be true to themselves, work hard, and still achieve greatness.

His lyrics became lessons for those who listened closely. He rapped about real life, about struggle and hope, about the importance of believing in yourself even when things seem impossible. His song *Alright* became a symbol of strength, reminding people that no matter what challenges they faced, they would make it through.

Kendrick also made it clear that success didn't mean forgetting where you came from. He stayed connected to Compton, visiting often and reminding young people that if he could make it, so could they. He was proof that a kid from a tough neighborhood could rise above the odds, chase his dreams, and inspire the world.

Beyond music, Kendrick's influence reached into culture, politics, and education. Colleges studied his lyrics as poetry. Leaders quoted his words in speeches. Young artists looked up to him as proof that hip-hop could be more than just entertainment, it could be a force for change.

For Kendrick, the greatest reward wasn't the awards or the fame. It was knowing that his music made a difference. That somewhere, a kid was picking up a notebook, writing their first rhyme, and believing that they too could be great.

Because of Kendrick Lamar, the next generation knew that their voices mattered. Their dreams were possible. And their stories were worth telling.

Chapter 7: Fun Facts & Cool Quotes

Kendrick Lamar isn't just one of the greatest rappers of all time, he's also a fascinating person with a unique journey. Here are some fun facts about him, along with some of his most powerful quotes that have inspired people all over the world.

Fun Facts About Kendrick Lamar

✏️ **His First Rap Name Was K-Dot**, Before using his real name, Kendrick went by the stage name "K-Dot." He released his first mixtape under that name, but later decided to be himself and rap as Kendrick Lamar.

📖 **He Was a Straight-A Student** – Even though he grew up in a tough neighborhood, Kendrick focused on his education. He did well in school, proving that hard work in the classroom was just as important as talent in music.

🎵 **He Saw Tupac and Dr. Dre Film a Music Video When He Was 8**, Kendrick's love for hip-hop started young, and seeing Tupac and Dr. Dre shoot the *California Love* music video in Compton made a huge impact on him.

🏆 **He's the First Rapper to Win a Pulitzer Prize**, His album *DAMN.* made history by becoming the first hip-hop album to ever win a Pulitzer Prize in music.

🎬 **He Created a Soundtrack for a Superhero Movie**, Kendrick produced and curated the soundtrack for *Black Panther* (2018), bringing his storytelling to the world of Marvel superheroes.

✏️ **He Freestyled for Over Two Hours Straight**, When Kendrick was younger, he once rapped non-stop for more than two hours at a recording session, showing his incredible talent and passion for hip-hop.

🎭 **He Made a Guest Appearance on a TV Show**, Kendrick acted in an episode of *Power*, a popular crime drama series, showing off his skills beyond music.

🏠 **He Stayed Humble Even After Fame**, Unlike many celebrities, Kendrick stayed true to his roots. Even after becoming famous, he didn't buy a giant mansion right away, he lived in a simple house and focused on his art.

Cool Quotes from Kendrick Lamar

💬 **"I'd rather not live like there isn't a God, then die and find out there really is."**, Kendrick often talks about faith in his music and life.

💬 **"If I'm gonna tell a real story, I'm gonna start with my name."**, This is why he chose to rap as Kendrick Lamar instead of using a stage name.

💬 **"We hurt because we're healed too."**, A reminder that growth comes from pain and experience.

💬 **"I'm not the next Tupac, I'm the first Kendrick Lamar."**, He respects legends like Tupac but always stays true to himself.

💬 **"Look inside my soul and you can find gold and maybe get rich."**, A powerful lyric from *Bitch, Don't Kill My Vibe* about self-worth and wisdom.

💬 **"Be different, do different things."**, A simple but powerful message about embracing individuality.

💬 **"We gon' be alright."**, From his song *Alright*, which became an anthem of hope and strength for many people.

Kendrick Lamar's story is proof that talent, hard work, and staying true to yourself can take you far. His music, wisdom, and success continue to inspire fans of all ages, showing that no matter where you come from, you have the power to make a difference.

CONCLUSION

Kendrick Lamar's story is more than just a tale of success, it's a journey of determination, creativity, and the power of staying true to yourself. From a quiet kid in Compton to one of the most influential voices in music, Kendrick has shown the world that dreams are worth chasing, no matter where you come from.

His music isn't just about catchy beats or clever lyrics. It's about storytelling, about capturing the truth of life, and about giving a voice to those who often go unheard. Through every song, every album, and every performance, Kendrick has shared his experiences, his struggles, and his hopes for a better world.

Kendrick's love for music started when he was just a boy, sitting in his room and listening to the greats. He filled notebooks with rhymes, using words to express what he saw and felt. While other kids played outside, he was crafting his future one lyric at a time.

Even as a young artist, he knew he wanted his music to be more than just entertainment. He wanted it to mean something. He wanted it to inspire. And that's exactly what he did.

Not every rapper uses their platform to make a difference, but Kendrick did. He didn't just rap about success, fame, or money. He rapped about real life, the struggles, the pain, the hope, and the joy of growing up in a world that wasn't always fair. He talked about the challenges young people face, especially in neighborhoods like Compton. He shared stories of hardship, but he also shared messages of hope.

One of the things that makes Kendrick special is that he never forgets where he came from. Even as he won awards, performed on the biggest stages, and became a global star, he stayed connected to his roots. He used his success to help others, giving back to his community and inspiring young people to follow their dreams.

Kendrick's career is filled with achievements that most artists only dream of. He released albums that were praised as masterpieces, won countless awards, and even made history by becoming the first rapper to win a Pulitzer Prize. His music became a voice for a generation, sparking conversations about important topics like race, justice, and self-worth.

When he produced the soundtrack for *Black Panther*, he brought his storytelling to the world of superheroes, proving that his talent went beyond rap. His song *Alright* became an anthem of hope, reminding people that no matter how hard life gets, they can push through.

Kendrick's story is proof that hard work, dedication, and belief in yourself can take you anywhere. He didn't have an easy path to success. He faced challenges, doubts, and struggles. But he never gave up. He kept writing, kept rapping, and kept pushing forward, even when things got tough.

For kids with big dreams, whether in music, sports, art, or anything else, Kendrick's journey is a reminder that success doesn't come overnight. It takes time, patience, and passion. It takes learning from mistakes and never giving up, even when things seem impossible.

Most importantly, Kendrick's story teaches us that we don't have to change who we are to be great. We can be quiet and thoughtful like Kendrick and still have a powerful voice. We can come from small places and still make a big impact. We can face challenges and still rise above them.

Kendrick's journey isn't over. Even after all he has accomplished, he continues to grow, evolve, and inspire. He keeps making music, keeps telling stories, and keeps using his voice to uplift others.

His legacy isn't just about the awards he's won or the records he's sold. It's about the way he has touched people's hearts and minds. It's about the kids who pick up a pen and start writing because they were inspired by his lyrics. It's about the people who listen to his music and feel understood.

As Kendrick once said, **"Be different, do different things."** His life is a perfect example of what happens when you embrace who you are, stay true to your passion, and never stop striving to make a difference.

If there's one thing to learn from Kendrick Lamar's story, it's that your dreams are possible. No matter where you come from, no matter what obstacles you face, you have the power to create your own future.

Maybe you love to write stories, draw pictures, play an instrument, or dream of becoming a scientist, an athlete, or an entrepreneur. Whatever your passion is, chase it. Work hard, stay focused, and believe in yourself.

Like Kendrick, you have a voice that matters. Your story is important. And the world is waiting to hear it.

Made in the USA
Monee, IL
30 March 2025

14881701R00030